# The Story

# of

# Charlwood Church

The Story of Charlwood Church
First published in the UK in 2022 by Stanford Publishing
Copyright © 2022 Stanford Publishing Limited
ISBN 978-1-999-3-555-5-5

The right of Brendon Sewill to be identified as the author has been asserted by him
in accordance with the Copyright, Designs and Patents Act, 1988.

Images of the Hassell paintings on pages 35, 36, 37 and 45 are reproduced by
permission of Surrey History Centre.

British Library Cataloguing in Publication Data. A catalogue record for this book is
available from the British Library.

Typeset in Avant Garde Gothic and Times New Roman
by Meriel Lewis, www.2m.org.uk

Printed in the UK by Cambrian Printers, www.pensordgroup.co.uk

Stanford Publishing Limited
24 Chapel Road
Stanford in the Vale
Faringdon
Oxfordshire
SN7 8LE
UK

Tel: +44 (0)1367 710677
Email: enquiries@stanfordpublishing.co.uk
Website: www.stanfordpublishing.co.uk

# Contents

# Preface

This book has grown out of four talks I gave in the winter of 2018 – 2019 on the history of Charlwood church. I started the talks by stating that I am not a historian. All my information comes from consulting various books and that *vade mecum*, the internet, and from intelligent deduction. I have been chairman of the church fabric committee for over thirty years and have therefore been fortunate to have been able to discuss the history of the church, as revealed in its architecture, with many experts. Unfortunately there are few written records relating specifically to Charlwood church; those that did exist, relating to recent periods, were destroyed in the Rectory fire of 1917.

An invaluable book has been *A Companion to the English Parish Church* 1996 by Stephen Friar, but foremost among my sources was *The Freemen of Charlwood* written by my mother Ruth Sewill, and her friend Elisabeth Lane, in 1950. For many of the documents they needed to consult, they had to travel to London, visit the Public Records Office, ask for the document, wait for it to be delivered and copy the relevant passages out by hand, much of which can now be done with a few clicks of the mouse.

I need to thank all those who have contributed photos, and Richard Astell of Stanford Publishing who has provided constant help and encouragement. Also the John Bristow and Thomas Mason Trust for covering the cost of publication. I hope that John Bristow, who became Rector in 1615, would be pleased with this account.

Brendon Sewill, 2022

*The Norman arch*

# Part 1: The Normans
# 1080 - 1280

The church of St Nicholas in Charlwood has two aisles. The North aisle of the church, the one furthest from the door, was built around 1080. Actually we don't know exactly when the church was built. There are no written records, and it is not mentioned in the Domesday Book (1086). Wooden buildings, like many old houses in Charlwood, can usually be dated by means of tree rings[1] but unfortunately there is no wood in the Norman part of the church, and no method has yet been invented to put a date on when stone is dug out of a quarry.

All we have is a fine Norman arch. According to the experts it is built in the Early Norman style, plain and undecorated. Early Norman arches were built sometime between 1066 and 1100.

The authors of *The Free Men of Charlwood* split the difference and called it circa 1080, and that date has stuck in local tradition. Indeed in 1980 we celebrated the church's 900th anniversary.

There is a great deal of Norman wall still standing. Many churches which claim to be Norman are merely built on Norman foundations, but in Charlwood the west wall, the north wall and all four walls of the tower – ground floor and first floor – are Norman.

In the north wall there is a small Norman slit window, built before glass became generally available. The other windows in the North aisle were added later, probably replacing small slit windows.

The walls, both the Norman ones and the later ones, are built in Charlwood stone, which is a local variety of Paludina limestone. The stone was probably dug out of the quarries in Edolph's Copse, on Stan Hill (originally Stone Hill) about half a mile away. It must have required a large labour force of Saxon peasants to dig the stone, to shape it, and to transport it to the building site before starting to build the church under the guidance, perhaps, of a Norman architect.

The quoins (corner stones) are made from Reigate stone.[2] This stone was easier to cut into square shapes but obviously further to transport. It is prone to erosion but has lasted well.

1

The church was extremely well built. The thick walls consist of an outer and an inner layer of stone with rubble in the middle. It stands on clay which when wet is soft and boggy. Yet despite fairly minimal foundations the walls and the tower have stood for over 900 years. In the 1980s the south wall, which was by comparison fairly modern being built soon after 1480, was beginning to lean outwards and had to be underpinned. But the walls built by the Normans have remained firm.

Indeed when the extension (the Nicholas Room) was built in 2009 the original foundations became visible: 5 or 6 feet of stone rubble. To meet modern building regulations, the new foundations had to be 12 feet deep with a solid concrete base and piles going down a further 12 feet!

## Similar churches

There are a couple of ancient churches in Sussex which may be similar to the original appearance of Charlwood church. Both are on the River Adur: in Norman times the river was an important port but has since silted up. The population has declined and therefore, unusually, the churches have not been extended.

The tower at Charlwood has an upper room (now with the bell-ropes, and called 'the ringing chamber') with a small window looking down the nave. Access must have been by ladder; the narrow circular stair being added at a later date.[3] The faint outline of a door can be identified on the outside of the northern wall.

*St Nicholas', Bramber.[4] Built 1071*

*St Botolph's, a few miles away, may be similar to the original appearance of Charlwood church*

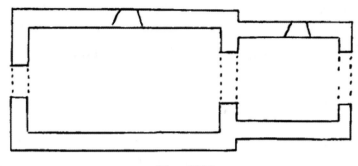

*Plan 1080*

Did the upper room provide living accommodation for the priest, or space for a bell? Or perhaps both? Perhaps with his wife (if she could face climbing the ladder): priests were not required to be celibate until after the Council of Trent in 1139. Perhaps after then with a concubine – an unmarried woman (although she would also have to have faced the ladder).

The plan above shows the church as originally built (now the north aisle). It is taken from *The Freemen of Charlwood* but amended and simplified. In particular a curved extension at the eastern end which indicated an apse has been deleted because, for reasons which are explained later, there is no evidence that there ever was an apse.

The church was originally thatched. The faint inverted V line on the tower shows the original roof line. Thatch requires a steeper pitch than tiles, to ensure that the rain runs off.

The patron saint of Charlwood church is Saint Nicholas. Many Norman churches seem to be dedicated to him, perhaps because he was the guardian of sailors, and blessed the Normans crossing the Channel.

Charlwood was attached to the manor of Merstham, and was a 'peculiar' of Canterbury priory. While other neighbouring parishes owed allegiance to Winchester, the

*Thatch roof line just visible*

3

responsibility for Charlwood was in the hands of the prior at Canterbury. When Henry VIII dissolved the monasteries in 1539, control passed to the King and thence to Winchester, then to Rochester, and finally to Southwark diocese when it was created in 1905.[5]

The church is listed by Historic England as Grade I – of national historic interest.

## Why was the church built here?

In the 11th century the Weald was an impenetrable mass of mud and brambles. So why did the Normans decide to build a church in Charlwood? It was a comparatively large church: with no pews and just a clay floor it could hold a congregation of over 100. The Domesday Book, compiled in 1085, does not mention Charlwood. Maybe Charlwood church had not been built by then, but one would still expect to find a sizeable settlement worthy of inclusion in such a comprehensive survey. The explanation given in various books on local history is that Charlwood was a sub-manor of Merstham (about eight miles north of Charlwood): but that explanation seems dubious.

The Domesday Book shows that the Archbishop of Canterbury held Merstham *'for himself, for the clothing of the monks. Before 1066 Merstham answered for 20 hides; now for 5 hides.'* A hide was about 120 acres, and the reduction in the area of farmland was probably a sign of the ravages caused by the Norman Conquest – indeed Merstham lay on the route taken by William's army from Canterbury to Winchester.

Merstham was recorded as having one church and a population of 21 villagers, 4 smallholders and 8 slaves (slavery was common in Saxon times but died out soon after the Conquest). It hardly looks likely that this included Charlwood.[6]

The Domesday Book does record the Norman church at Betchworth, but Betchworth had a lord to finance the building of the church: there was no lord at Charlwood. The Saxon church a few miles away at Worth is also included. The records show that it was built sometime between 950 and 1050 to serve a royal hunting lodge: but there was no hunting lodge at Charlwood.

A Mesolithic site c.4,000 BC has been found about half a mile away on the edge of Glovers Wood. The site – on dry ground near the stream – is similar to the location of the church. Thus there may have been a village here since prehistoric times.

In Saxon times Charlwood may have had a small wooden church. On our clay soil remains of wooden buildings are unlikely to remain, but perhaps the slightly raised ground in the churchyard to the east of the old yew tree marks the site of the Saxon church. The yew has been dated at about a hundred years older than the present church.

Perhaps Charlwood had a prosperity based on iron. There is a piece of iron slag (a by-product of the smelting process) in the west wall of the church, built in c.1280. There were Roman iron works at Bewbush, three miles south; and a medieval ironworks at Ewood, three miles west. There were ironworks all over Sussex and the southern part of Surrey. Charlwood is not listed in the classic study *Wealden Iron*[7] but does get a brief mention in the more recent *The Iron Industry of the Weald*.[8] There are a few old field names which may indicate mining. The remains of a bay (dam) and silted up pond at the end of Glovers Road are probably medieval.

Another theory is that the church was built for the forest people – all the people who lived in the woods, making a living from cutting timber and making charcoal. Maybe Charlwood got its name from the charcoal burning. Certainly the footpaths, which tend to date from Saxon times, lead straight to the church from Ifield, Newdigate, Ockley and Leigh.[9] But that would not explain the large labour force needed to build the church, nor who paid for it. The experts, however, say that the name is derived from Ceorl wood, the wood of the free men: men who owed no allegiance to a lord.[10]

Another speculation is that Charlwood was a centre for Saxon resistance to the Normans, and that in around 1080 the Normans rounded up the rebels and put them to work building the church. It is given in the Appendix on page 52.

## Thomas Becket

The first written record we have is that the vicar of Charlwood was excommunicated by Archbishop Thomas Becket on Christmas Day 1170.

> *'Then, after the customary prayers for the pope and the peace*
> *and prosperity of the people, he excommunicated all violators of*

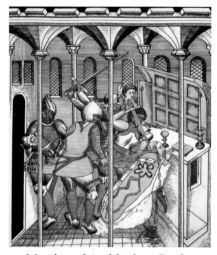

*Murder of Archbishop Becket*

*the rights of his church and the fomentors of discord in general, and named Robert and Randulf de Broc and the vicars Intruded into Charlwood and Harrow ... May they all be damned by Jesus Christ he intoned as he hurled the flaming candles to the floor.'[11]*

Four days later, Thomas was murdered in the cathedral.

The background to this event is that Archbishop Thomas Becket fell out with King Henry II, and was exiled to France for six years. When he was permitted to return, on 1 December 1170, some Norman knights (such as Randulf de Broc) and clerics (such as his brother Robert de Broc, archdeacon of Canterbury) refused to recognise his authority.

What does this incident tell us about Charlwood? That Charlwood was a comparatively important place, worth an archbishop fussing about.

## The rood screen

At some time between 1100 and 1500 a rood screen was erected in front of the Norman arch. The purpose of the screen was partially to fence off the chancel where the priest performed the miracle of transubstantiation, transforming the bread and wine into the body and blood of Christ. The host, as it was called, was then brought out and held aloft to the wonderment of the peasant congregation.[12]

Above the screen was a wooden platform, called the rood loft, on which mystery plays were performed, the players appearing as if by magic. In the Protestant reformation, a Privy Council Order in 1548 declared rood screens and rood lofts to be a Catholic superstition, and ordered them all to be removed. Only a few rare examples remain, such as that illustrated opposite.

*The rood screen at Swimbridge, Devon*

The rood screen which used to be situated in the north aisle should not be confused with the existing screen in the south aisle. The latter did not fall foul of the Protestant prohibition: it fenced off a private chapel and thus did not have a religious significance.

In Charlwood there is a slight indent in the wall above and to the right of the Norman arch. In 2018 removal of the plaster in the ringing chamber revealed a blocked doorway which would have given access to the rood loft.

*The blocked door of the rood loft, discovered in 2018. The black streak is where render has been added at a later time.*

# Part 2. The Plantagenet Period
## 1280 - 1480

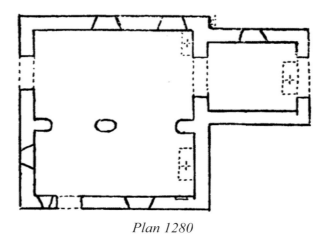

*Plan 1280*

In about 1280 a chapel was built onto the south-west side of the church – it is now the part of the church between the main south door and the pulpit.

There were two manors in Charlwood: Charlwood Place (now Lory's farm) occupied by the Saunders family, and Gatwick Manor (the manor house site is now under the Gatwick north terminal). There was also – later – a smaller manor of the Rectory.

Research by the late Patrick Billinghurst indicated that the chapel was probably built by the de Gatwicke family who lived at Gatwick manor.[13] John de Gatwicke is recorded as living there in 1304 (and left it to his daughter and her husband Thomas de Cobham), thence to the Jordan family.

To put the chapel into historic context, it was built soon after the final crusade. It is possible that a member of the de Gatwicke family died on a crusade; and that the chapel was built to enable prayers to be said for his soul. The figure of the knight in the wall-painting supports this theory.

There was a wall across what is now the south aisle, and an altar against the wall. That is indicated

*The piscina*

by the piscina (for washing the communion vessels) behind the pulpit. It is thought that the design, with the water draining into the foundations, was to prevent witches obtaining the consecrated wine.

## The wall paintings

The paintings on the south wall date from the time that this chapel was built, that is around 1280 or soon after. They are among the finest wall paintings in Britain; are almost older than the earliest English painting in the National Gallery, and are unusual in telling graphic short stories rather than scenes from the Bible or the Last Judgement.

It should always be remembered that in medieval times these paintings would have been, not artistic decorations, but objects of reverence, adoration and prayer.

A careful comparison of the costumes has revealed that they were all painted at around the same time. Covered with whitewash at the Reformation in around 1550, when the Protestants did not approve of any portrayal of saints, the wall paintings were rediscovered in 1858.

*The wall paintings*

A travelling painter, perhaps trained in a monastery, would have been hired to decorate the freshly plastered walls. In his bag he would have carried, not only brushes and pigments, but also scrolls of illustrations of potential paintings. Once the subject was chosen, the painter would set to work to enlarge his small original. Traces of lines, vertical and horizontal, still remain. Their survival is probably due to the lines having been drawn using a pigmented string held taut against the fresh plaster. Onto a preparatory layer of limewash the painter then sketched out the main outlines in red ochre, filling in using red and yellow ochre, amber, charcoal black and limewhite.

Since the 1860s various attempts have been made to restore and preserve the paintings, with various degrees of success. In 1993 experts from the Canterbury wall-paintings workshop removed previous layers of varnish and accumulated dirt. In accordance with current archaeological practice they were not permitted to touch up any of the paintings.

At the same time an art historian, Ann Worrall, was commissioned to paint a picture of the murals as they would have looked when first painted 700 years ago, using the paints available at that time. This picture hangs at the back of the church.

The two shields above the window probably indicate who it was who commissioned the paintings. They are not entirely dissimilar to the coat of arms now offered for sale to those with the name 'Gatwick'.

*Ann Worrall's facsimile of the wall painting as it was when first created*

*The knight*

Above the window is a knight in armour, not connected to the religious themes of the other paintings. Perhaps he was the member of the de Gatwicke family who was killed on a crusade. The red and white stripes of his shield and banner may be connected to Pope Gregory X (1271-76) who was the first to wear red and white vestments.

Who was the small boy running across the top of the window? He is very indistinct and may be no more than a figment of Ann Worrall's imagination.

## The story of St Margaret

The painting to the left of the pulpit tells the story of St Margaret, one of the most widely venerated saints of the early Church. She was the guardian of women in childbirth and hers was one of the 'voices' that spoke to Joan of Arc. In the modern idiom, she was an early 'Me Too' character, an innocent girl dominated and abused by a wealthy and influential man.

The painting shows Margaret sitting demurely spinning wool as she minded her sheep. The pagan governor of Antioch, Olibrius, is out hunting, with his greyhound in pursuit of a hare. This is believed to be the earliest picture of a greyhound in England.

*St Margaret*

Behind him is his huntsman, blowing his horn. In front strides a herald bearing his master's standard, sent to ask Margaret's hand in marriage – or perhaps a more immediate assignment! Margaret was, however, a good Christian, and firmly said 'no'.

In the centre row of the painting Margaret is seen being cruelly beaten, the faces of her torturers being painted with ugly features to show their evil status, and then thrown into prison. The devil arrives in the form of a dragon and tempts her to end her sufferings by submitting to the lord's desire. She, however, resists temptation and is shown being swallowed by the devil-dragon – although with the hand of God above.

In the lowest tier of the painting Margaret is depicted emerging from the dragon having made the sign of the cross in its belly. She is shown in her traditional pose standing triumphant over its body, staff in hand.

The final scene (bottom right) depicts her martyrdom. A judge orders her to death. The huge sword of the executioner was a symbol of medieval justice. He holds her head by her hair prior to decapitation. The dove flying heavenward, however, represents her innocent soul flying up to heaven.

This sad end to the story appears somewhat inconsequential but was explained by a French preacher in 1681 as showing God's respect for the system of justice. More likely it merely shows that in medieval times when the local lord was also the judge, it was a mistake to thwart his wishes.

In the wall painting the head of the judge is missing. Ann Worral, however, used some artistic licence to copy the head of Olibrius from the top panel. That was not irrational. As a twelfth-century writer recorded:

> *'Meanwhile, the English were groaning under the Norman yoke ... the [Norman lords] were so swollen with pride that they would not deign to hear the reasonable plea of the English or give them impartial judgement. When their men at arms were guilty of plunder and rape they protected them by force, and wreaked their wrath all the more violently upon those who complained of the cruel wrongs they suffered.'[14]*

## St Nicholas and the Three Boys

To the right of the pulpit the upper painting shows the miraculous resuscitation by St Nicholas, the patron saint of Charlwood church, of three scholars who had been cut up and salted for pork. The pork butcher and his wife stand to the left, looking evil, with St Nicholas to the right. Above the boys the hand of God emerges from a starry cloud.[15] St Nicholas was the patron saint of children (as well as of sailors, prostitutes, brewers, and pawnbrokers).

Another story about St Nicholas is how he threw three bags of gold into the window of a house to provide dowries to enable three girls to marry. That story is commemorated by three black discs on the weather vane (1980) on the church tower.

## The Three Living and The Three Dead

The lower painting is of the Three Living and the Three Dead. This story is taken from an old French *moralité* written c.1290. It relates how three noble youths hunting in a forest are met by three hideous spectres, images of death, from whom they receive a lecture on the vanity of human grandeur. The skeletons utter an early soundbite: '*As you are, we were; as we are, you will be.*'

This subject is found in fourteen other churches in England, but this is the only one where the princes, wearing crowns, are on horses. Two of the princes

13

*Detail showing St Nicholas, the Living and the Dead, and the Archer*

have hawks on their wrists. It was much in use at the time of the Black Death in 1348 but the Charlwood picture may have been painted before then.

It has been surmised that this picture was painted by a different painter than that of St Margaret. In that picture the paint-work never crosses the horizontal lines, but here St Nicholas' feet intrude on the lower painting.

Both the story of St Margaret and that of the three princes appear slightly anti-establishment. Olibrius can be seen as a Norman knight behaving in a shameful way, while the three skeletons seem to tell the Norman knights that they will get their comeuppance. So why did the de Gatwicke family, with their Norman name, wish to distance themselves from the Norman rulers?

## The Archer

In the 1400s the paintings to the right of the pulpit were covered in limewash, and a large new painting, of the martyrdom of St Edmund, was superimposed.

Edmund, born 841, was King of the East Angles. In a great battle against the Danes in 869 he was captured, tied to a tree and shot with arrows until his

*Martyrdom of St Edmund, Church of St Peter and St Paul, Pickering*

body was 'like a thistle covered with prickles'. Edmund was soon revered as a martyr, and his body was enshrined at Bury St Edmunds.

In the Charlwood painting there is now no sign of St Edmund: only the archer remains (but without his arrow).[16] A clue to the date of the painting is that the archer's shoes are of a type that remained in fashion until the 1480s. It is fascinating that the archer is almost identical to the archers in a painting of St Edmund in Pickering, North Yorkshire, which is dated as c.1450. It is a mystery that, in the Charlwood painting when the whitewash was removed in 1858, it was possible to remove all traces of Edmund, and parts of the bow and arrow, leaving the earlier paintings intact. Was perhaps Edmund never painted?[17]

There are signs that there may also have been a painting of St Christopher, above the door. That was the traditional place for the patron saint of travellers.

## Windows

In the western end of the part of the church added in 1280 there are two tall lancet windows in the Early English style, a development of the Norman slit window as seen on the north wall.

15

An important advance in architecture can, however, be seen in the window on the south wall, to the right of the pulpit. This consisted of putting two lancet windows side-by-side, in a design described as 'a rare example of plate tracery'.[18]

A similar window was added a few years later (c.1300?) in the north wall. On the outside it has two small faces, now much eroded, carved in the dripstone – the stone ridge around the window. The glass for these windows may have come from Chiddingfold where a glass works was recorded in a deed of 1280.[19]

## The door

The main wooden door of the church also dates from around 1280. It is a remarkable piece of wood to have lasted over 700 years. The upper iron hinge is of this date, and is made from local iron.

The door is in the traditional position on the south side of the church. It suggests that this part of the church could not have been built as a semi-private chantry chapel – everyone would have to walk through the chapel to get to the main aisle.

*The door*

## The new chancel

The next stage of building was the construction in around 1330 of a new chancel, now the vestry.[20] Its large glass windows – the right-hand one (from inside) on the north side is original – would have let the sunlight in from three sides; it would have provided an attractive setting for the altar compared to its previous dark position under the tower.

The old chancel has a fine roof – after the door the oldest piece of woodwork in the church.[21] Grooves can be seen

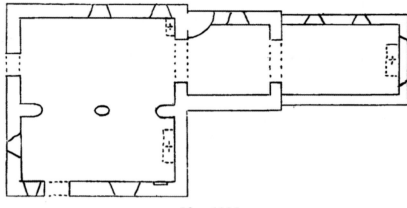

*Plan 1330*

in the rafters to hold boards to give the ceiling a flat surface, possibly at one time painted or plastered although no traces remain.

We need to remind ourselves that the altar stood here from around 1330 to around 1880. On either side of the altar were two niches for the statues of saints. The statues were demolished in the Protestant Reformation in 1550, along with the small platforms on which they stood. But an account written in 1841 records that the niches 'were found ornamentally painted in blue and red, the colours quite fresh'.[22]

## Was there an apse?

Some Victorian books, and *The Freemen of Charlwood*, suggested that when Charlwood church was first built, in c.1080, it had an apse, that is a semi-circular addition to the eastern end, designed to amplify the voice of the

*St Nicholas' Church, Worth, with its large apse*

priest.[23] That was the standard design of Romanesque Norman churches. It was assumed to have been demolished to make space for the new chancel.

There are, however, no architectural or archaeological indications of an apse (although any archaeological evidence would be under the floor of the present vestry). It seems likely that there never was an apse and that Charlwood originally looked like St Nicholas', Bramber, or the nearby St Botolph's, illustrated above on page 2.

This issue leads on to the question of the further, eastern-most, arch – the one beyond the Norman arch. It is clearly Norman in shape but has deteriorated, and has had to be repaired by iron bands and cement.

It may originally have been what is called a 'blind arch', framing small windows. Again the church at Bramber (c.1071) provides a possible example. The main arch is very similar to that in Charlwood, and beyond the altar there is a blind arch enclosing three small Norman windows.

*St Nicholas', Bramber, showing the Norman arch and the blind arch beyond*

If this explanation is correct, then in Charlwood, when the new chancel was added in c.1330, the blind arch was modified to become a full – but not very strong – Norman-shaped round arch.

In attempting to unravel the history of Charlwood church there is another mystery. When the plaster was removed from the eastern wall of the ringing chamber in the tower in 2018, the remains of an unfinished and blocked up arch were discovered. It is immediately over the further 'Noman' arch, and is shown in the picture opposite.

The shape of the mystery arch, and thus its date, has not been established. Nor its purpose. Was it to let light into the new chancel? – but not much light was available in the ringing chamber. Was it to let light into the ringing chamber? – not necessary. Perhaps it was originally planned as a great east window to let light into the old and dark chancel under the tower (assuming no floor to the ringing chamber) but was then abandoned when they built the new chancel instead. But why is it such rough undressed and uncarved stone?

*The mystery arch in the ringing chamber*

# Part 3. The Tudors
# 1480 - 1600

The next major addition to the church was made as a result of the death of Richard Saunders in 1480. He tragically died aged only 30. His widow, Agnes, planned the extension of the south aisle and the creation of a chantry chapel in the area beyond the screen, where the altar and the choir stalls now stand.

In those days it was believed that when a person died, their soul went into purgatory where it had to be purged of all sins. If a priest could say daily prayers the soul would ascend to heaven more quickly.

The Saunders family lived at Charlwood Place, and owned most of the land in Charlwood. They allocated the rent of one farm to pay the priest (11 shillings) and for the relief of poverty (3 shillings).[24] The farm was called '*Chantry Silver*'. After four hundred years the name survives: the farm at Norwood Hill is still called '*Chantersluer*'.

Richard's tomb would have stood in the centre of the chantry chapel (remember the altar was in what is now the vestry). We do not know what it looked like but it was probably similar to the tomb (shown below) of Prince Arthur (elder brother of Henry VIII) in the chantry chapel at Worcester cathedral.

Richard's father, William Saunders, died soon afterwards, in 1481. His body might have been added to the tomb. He had married Johanna Carew, a rich heiress, so funds were not short for building the chantry chapel.

Richard's widow, Agnes, was a local girl: she is recorded as having been born in Charlwood. But sadly she too died young, on 7 January, 1485. The building of the chantry chapel was left to her young son, Nicholas.

Around the time that the chapel was being completed, and the new hammer-beam roof built, Christopher Columbus discovered America.

*Prince Arthur's tomb*

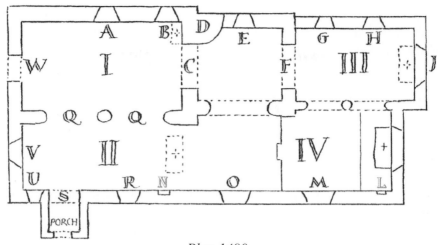

*Plan 1480*

| | | | |
|---|---|---|---|
| I. | Built in c.1080 | II. | Built in c.1280 |
| III. | Built in c.1330 | IV. | Built in c.1480 |

| | | | |
|---|---|---|---|
| A. | Norman window | B. | Window c.1300 and altar ? |
| C. | Early Norman arch | D. | Circular stair to tower |
| E. | Window under tower | F. | Norman arch, formerly blind? |
| G. | Window; date unknown | H. | Window c.1330 |
| J. | Window c.1480 | L. | Saunders' brass |
| M. | Tudor window c.1480 | N. | Piscina c.1280 |
| O. | Tudor window c.1480 | Q. | Arches, date unknown |
| R. | Window c.1280 | S. | South door c.1280 |
| U. | Window, Early English c.1280 | V. | Window, Early English c.1280 |
| W. | West door, probably rebuilt in c.1480 when window enlarged | | |

In the plan above, taken from *The Freemen of Charlwood*, I have put a date of 1480 against a number of items because that is when Richard Saunders died, and when the chantry chapel would have been planned. But, of course, it would have taken a few years to construct.

## Building the new chapel

When the building work was completed, perhaps around 1500, the wall across the church by the current pulpit was knocked down with, perhaps, the loss of

21

a few inches of the wall-painting of St Margaret.[25] The altar against this wall would have been removed. The wall between the new chantry chapel and the altar was also demolished, being replaced by two arches in typical Tudor double-headed style.[26]

The new chantry chapel and the extension of the south aisle were built in local Charlwood stone so that, externally, it is hard to see where the new joins the old. The two large windows in the extension are, however, built in Tudor style with flat, not arched, tops.

The other large, but arched, windows in the church – the east window over the present altar, the east window in the present vestry, and the window at the west end of the north aisle – are all thought to date from this time, around 1500.

It is not known when the two arches between the south aisle and the north aisle were built (marked Q, see plan of 1480). The roof is suspended on a slender stone pillar (now leaning at a somewhat perilous angle). They are, however, very similar to the third arch, that nearest the screen, which was obviously constructed when the south aisle was extended in the years after 1480.

## The roof

The magnificent hammer beam roof dates from the time of the chantry chapel, the opportunity being taken to roof the whole of the south aisle. The north aisle has an identical hammer beam roof. Some history books suggest that this may be earlier, because that type of roof was typical of the previous century, but it seems more likely that the whole church was re-roofed in the years after 1480.

Originally the roofs would have been thatched. At a later date the roofs of both aisles were entirely made of Horsham slabs (still excavated today from a quarry near Horsham). In the 1800s most of this heavy stone was removed, apart from the three lower courses, and replaced by clay tiles.

## The screen

The medieval screen, which enclosed the chantry chapel, is one of the glories of Charlwood church.

*The screen*

When it was first erected, however, it did not have the colourful top panel (the cornice): only the delicately carved pattern of the vine with the small initials 'RS' for Richard Saunders. The vine was frequently used as a Christian symbol.[27] The cornice is in three sections, probably because it was made elsewhere, and transported to Charlwood. It is decorated in gesso, a type of plaster, and does not fit exactly above the screen.

The centre panel features the initials 'IHS' – the first three letters of Jesus in Greek – and a crowned 'M' for the Virgin Mary.

Also, on each side, are the arms of the Saunders family – the three bulls (heads and red tongues) – and the arms of the Carew family – the three lions, now rather indistinct. This would have been Richard's coat of arms, representing his father's and his mother's families.

*The centre panel*

*Saunders' family arms*

The two outer panels contain the initials 'RS', to commemorate Richard Saunders, each repeated twice and supported by griffins.

It is sometimes suggested that this cornice was made to decorate the Saunders' private pew, after the tomb had been removed.[28] But it was more likely to have been around the tomb, perhaps with a fourth side, now lost.

Each of the panels is six feet long. Six feet for the centre panel would seem rather wide for the end of the tomb (but equally wide for the end of the pew). It would imply that the tomb was square, perhaps because it contained the bodies of Richard, his wife Agnes and his father William. Yet the panels have only Richard's initials.

The cornice was not always on top of the screen. The crown on the Virgin Mary would not have pleased the Protestants, so perhaps when the tomb was removed the panels had to go into hiding. It was not there when John Aubrey wrote his history of Surrey in 1719 but it was there when Manning and Bray wrote in 1808.[29]

The cornice was re-painted in its original colours by churchwarden Richard Venables in 1970. He did this without permission from the diocese during an Interregnum when there was no Rector to get into trouble. A faculty would never have been granted – the rule is that historic features must not be touched up – but the result of his work is magnificent.

## The porch

In medieval England, church porches were used for a variety of rites: announcing the banns of marriage; exchanging rings before the wedding service; the churching of women; and the first part of the baptism service. Girls who had committed fornication (but not the boys) attended in white sheets to seek absolution. It is not known if any of these ceremonies took place in Charlwood but the stone

*The porch*

seats in the porch seem to suggest that an audience was expected.

Most history books suggest that the porch was added in around 1480, at the same time that the extension of the south aisle was built. But its method of construction seems to put this in doubt. The lowest three feet of wall is made of Charlwood stone: perhaps it originally supported a wooden porch.

The main part of the porch walls is of Wealden sandstone. The nearest quarry is at West Hoathly about ten miles away, and there is no nearer outcrop of sandstone. This suggests that the porch was constructed at a time when the quarries on Stan Hill were not in operation, perhaps in the 1400s. Finally the front triangle of the porch is made of brick which indicates a later date.

There are various graffiti on the walls. One has the date AD sixteen hundred and something. The front of the porch has curved indentations which puzzle most visitors: they were where men who were cutting the churchyard sharpened their scythes. It also contains an Ordnance Survey bench mark, dated 1921, which shows that the church is 221.6 feet above sea level.

## The Reformation

King Edward was only 9 when he came to the throne in 1547, and died when he was 15. Yet his reign saw huge changes in the official religion – the change from Catholic to Protestant. All were reflected in the architecture of Charlwood church.

*The stoup*

**The chantry chapel** was converted into a private pew for the Saunders family. Protestants felt it wrong that anyone could get to Heaven more quickly just by paying the priest to say regular prayers. A law banning chantry chapels was passed in 1549.

**The tomb** was removed and the ornamental cornice put into hiding or, perhaps, used to decorate the Saunders pew. What happened to the bodies in the tomb? They would never have been buried in the tomb but in the ground under it. They are probably still there.

**The statues** on either side of the altar were destroyed. The Protestants did not believe in praying to saints. The niches in what is now the vestry remain but the small platforms, on which the statues stood, have gone.

**The wall paintings** were covered in lime-wash, and not re-discovered for over 300 years.

**The Holy Water stoup**, in the porch, was probably broken at this time.

**The stone altar**, if there was one, was replaced by a simple wooden table. Most parishes had a stone altar, so the chances are that Charlwood had one. Some parishes, hoping for a return of Catholicism, buried their altars but in Charlwood one has never been found.

**The windows**, if they contained stained-glass images of the saints, were smashed, and replaced by plain glass. But a few fragments of the old glass were re-used, and can still be seen in the top panels of four windows.

**Rood screen**. Out went the Catholic belief in transubstantiation, that the bread and wine were miraculously turned into the body and blood of Christ, replaced by the belief that they were eaten and drunk in remembrance of Him. And with this change, out went the Rood Screens, removed by Order of the Privy Council in 1548. In future the actions of the clergy were no longer to be hidden from view.

**Church valuables**. Another effect of the reformation was the seizure for the King of all the rich copes and communion vessels that the church had accumulated over four hundred years. The excuse was that, in the new Protestant faith, religion should be simple with no need for Rome-ish finery yet, as with the suppression of the monasteries twenty-five years previously, the King was glad to have the money.

The list of all the church possessions in Charlwood was drawn up by Commissioners, including Sir Thomas Saunders (grandson of Richard) in 1552. The full list, and also the much smaller list of what the church was permitted to keep, is given in full in *The Freemen of Charlwood*.

Was Charlwood particularly susceptible to this iconoclastic orgy? Probably yes, because Sir Thomas Saunders had become the 'King's Remembrancer', that is the chief legal officer with the task of remembering, and enforcing, the King's commands throughout Britain. If his home village had not complied, Thomas's job – and perhaps his life – would have been on the line.[30]

*The Freemen of Charlwood* suggests that all these alterations may have taken place during the Puritan regime in 1640-60, but it seems more likely that they occurred during the time of Thomas Saunders when one can deduce a real personal connection and motive.

## The pulpit

While so much was removed or destroyed, there is one fine reminder of the Reformation in Charlwood church, and that is the pulpit.

Its fine Tudor linenfold panelling shows that it dates from around this time, perhaps from 1547 when King Edward VI ordered that every parish should provide 'a comely and honest pulpit'. In accordance with the new belief that the gospel should be preached

*The pulpit*

to all the people, with the Bible in English, the pulpit, and lectern, is placed at the only place in the church – half-way down the south aisle – that commands a view of all (or almost all) the congregation.[31]

## The Saunders' brass

In July 1553 Mary became Queen, and Britain became Roman Catholic again. All legislation passed by King Edward was repealed. Sir Thomas Saunders, no doubt as a result of some quick political footwork, retained his position as Remembrancer. But there are no signs of this temporary end of the Reformation in the architecture of the church.

In Charlwood the big event, soon after the accession of Mary, was the death of Nicholas Saunders, son of Richard, father of Thomas, at the age of 70. During his life as squire of Charlwood he had overseen the extension of the south aisle and the building of the chantry chapel. He and his wife, and their four sons and six daughters, are commemorated in the fine brass situated to the right of the altar.

*The Saunders' brass*

The inscription (which one suspects that Thomas, with some pride, wrote) reads:

> *'Here is buried Nicholas Saunders Esquyer and Alys his Wyfe daughter of John Hungate of the Countey of Yorke Esquyer Father and Mother of Thomas Saunder knight ye kyng remembrance of thxcheker which Nicholas deceased the xxix day of August in ye first yere of ye Reigne of queene Mary'.*

Note that Nicholas is described as 'Esquyer' and not as 'Knight'. And curiously Thomas describes himself as King's Remembrance[r] not as the Queen's Remembrance[r].

The central diamond is rather fun. It shows a bull apparently chewing a stick of celery. The bull was the emblem of the Saunders family. It is actually chewing a bunch of alisaundre (horse parsley), a plant then used instead of celery. In the family their mother's name, Alys Saunders, had obviously been slurred to become a nickname 'Alisaundre' – like calling her 'Celery'. A good joke 460 years old!

## The Helmet

The helmet that hangs above the altar is a replica of a funeral helmet that was carried on the coffin of either Nicholas Saunders or Thomas Saunders. It was stolen in 1973, eventually recovered and deposited with Guildford Museum for safekeeping. A group of volunteers, with a grant from the Heritage Fund, commissioned a young Charlwood blacksmith to make an exact replica which was placed in the church in January 2020.

*The Freemen of Charlwood* states firmly that the helmet was used at the funeral of Nicholas in 1553.[32]

*Replica of the stolen funeral helmet*

29

But Nicholas may not have been knighted, and the helmet may date from the funeral of Sir Thomas in 1563.

Thomas certainly had had a remarkable life, arranging the divorce of Henry VIII from Anne of Cleves, dealing with the legal fall-out from Catherine Howard's execution; being elected as an MP; and acting as 'enforcer' for the violent religious changes of Henry, Edward, Mary and finally Elizabeth.

## The liturgy

Many of the prayers still used in the church services in Charlwood were written or revised by Archbishop Thomas Cranmer (1489 - 1556). Noted for his beautiful English prose, the *Book of Common Prayer* reflects protestant beliefs and was brought into use in 1549. Banned when Britain reverted to Catholicism under Queen Mary (and poor Archbishop Cranmer burned at the stake), the Book was reissued by Queen Elizabeth in 1559.

## Queen Elizabeth I

In 1558 when Queen Elizabeth I came to the throne, Charlwood church was about 478 years old. Since then, 464 years have passed.

After the religious turmoil of the reigns of Henry VIII, Edward and Mary, Queen Elizabeth introduced a period of peace and compromise, setting the pattern for what is today the Church of England. The evidence of that compromise is in the liturgy used at the standard communion service where the sacraments are given with the words: "The body of our Lord Jesus Christ…" (the implication that the bread has become the actual body of Jesus thus pleasing those of a Catholic disposition). *"Take and eat in remembrance that Christ died for you …."* (thus pleasing the Protestants who did not believe in transubstantiation).

## The Muniment Chest

Another feature of the church which has existed since Tudor times is the muniment chest.

It is not known if this dates from around 1538, when Thomas Cromwell ordered all parishes to keep a 'secure coffer' as a repository for the register of all weddings, baptisms, deaths; or from 1595 when the existing Charlwood register begins.

As well as the registers, the chest was used for keeping all the church valuables – the rich copes and the gold communion vessels. As was traditional, the chest has three locks so that the rector and two church wardens had to be present when it was opened.

When Ruth Sewill came to write *The Freemen of Charlwood* she found that the chest contained all the invoices for the Charlwood workhouse (now part of the Kitchen Shop) dating from about 1750 - 1830, when the churchwardens were also the Overseers of the Poor.[33]

*The muniment chest*

# Part 4. The Modern Age
## 1600 – Today

In 1600 the Rector was Michael Earle. When he died in 1615 he left land in Sussex the rent of which was to be paid each year to the poor: *'forty shillings of lawful money of England at or in the portche of the Parrish Church of Charlewood upon the Feaste day of St Michaell tharchangell'*. Earle's charity still exists and still helps the poor of Charlwood.

He was succeeded as Rector by John Bristow. He built what is now known as 'Bristow's Cottage' as the village school which it remained until 1850. When he died in 1637 he donated land in Beggarhouse Lane to provide for the free education of three Charlwood children from poor families – other parents had to pay. The rent of the cottage now accrues to Bristow's Charity which in 1999 was amalgamated with another (rather richer) charity to become the John Bristow and Thomas Mason Trust. That trust, which now has a capital of over £2 million, has done much to help preserve the fabric of the church.[34]

The Jordan family had lived at Gatwick Manor in Charlwood since 1300. Two of their descendants, John Shelley and Colin Gates, still live in the village. A brass plaque on the wall of what was the chancel, now the vestry, records (in Latin):

> *Here lies William Jordan of Gatwick, gentleman, who died 7th May 1625, and Katherine his wife, only daughter and joint heir of Laurence Hussey, Doctor of Laws, master of the Chancellery and envoy to the Queen of Scotland; which Laurence was son and heir of Antony Hussey, agent of the Queen of England in Germany and overseer of transactions of English merchants in Belgium and Moscovy; which Katherine died 30 January 1626.*

Katherine was obviously proud of her father and grandfather! Indeed the Jordan family had become a good deal richer than the Saunders family of Charlwood Place. They obviously felt it unjust that the Saunders should have possession of their grand family pew, and moved in to take occupation of three seats. This created a major row which culminated in 1638 in legal action over *'the liberty to set and bury in the Chapell'*. The result of arbitration was to award the Jordan family the right *'to sitt in the three seats in the said Chappell or Isle wherein the sd. Edmund Jordan his wife and Children have used to Sitt.'*

*The line where additional height was added to the tower
after the Restoration is clearly visible*

The row must have caused much embarrassment for Thomas Mulcaster who, in 1637 at the age of 28, had become Rector; especially as he had married Philippa Saunders of Charlwood Place.

## The civil war

This 'civil war' in Charlwood was soon followed by the Civil War in England which began in 1642. The Rector and the Saunders family presumably supported the King while most of the people of Charlwood, like the majority of South East England, probably supported Parliament. An account, obviously written by a Royalist, tells how Thomas Mulcaster was proceeded against by 'five or six of the very scum of the parish', and retired to Mitcham 'in Danger of his Life'.[35]

The Saunders family, as lords of the manor, were unpopular. It was probably at this time that their grand house, Charlwood Place, was burnt down. A monument in the south aisle to William and Joan Saunders was removed;[36] so also an inscription in the porch which stated (in Latin):

*Pray for the souls of Thomas Sander and Joan his wife and for the souls of all the faithful departed.*[37]

There are no records of the Puritan regime in Charlwood. The Puritans believed in 'purifying' religion to get rid of any remaining superstitions, anything that was not mentioned in the Bible. An Act of Parliament required all altars and altar rails to be demolished. Musical instruments were banned; however, singing the psalms unaccompanied was considered appropriate.

Baptisms, weddings and funerals were not permitted in church. In other times, a record of these events was kept in the parish register in the church. There are, however, no entries in the Charlwood register from 1634 until 1650; and again from 1653 to 1660.[38]

The somewhat miserable Puritans also tried to ban what were 'vulgarly called Holy Days' such as Christmas but this proved controversial and was not implemented everywhere.

## The Restoration

In 1660 the Puritan era ended with the Restoration of the monarchy. Charles II became king, and Thomas Mulcaster was reappointed as Rector of Charlwood. Almost immediately the tower of Charlwood church was raised, with the new addition clearly visible (and proving again the strength of the Norman foundations). It was built of Charlwood stone, to match the rest of the church. The decorative battlements were probably added at this time.

*The new bells*

New bells were installed, the previous bells having presumably been melted down to make cannons.

No time was lost. Bell number 6 is inscribed "William Eldridge made mee 1662." The other five bells are dated 1667, 1668, two in 1764, and 1835.

## Two hundred peaceful years

The two hundred years from 1660 to 1860 were relatively calm and tranquil. There were no architectural changes in Charlwood church.

In 1791 the Churchwardens, John Saunders and GV Jackson, erected a sundial on the front of the porch, inscribed with the date MDCCXCI.[39]

Clearly the Saunders family still played a large part in chuch affairs but those who were not 'gentry' increasingly felt happier in nonconformist chapels. Tanyard Farm continued as a Quaker meeting house as it had been since the 1600s; and in 1815 a local farmer, Joseph Flint, purchased a redundant army barracks in Horsham and re-erected it in Charlwood as a non-denominational chapel. By 1850 it had a congregation almost as large as the church.

## The Hassel Paintings

In 1820 John Hassell painted a number of pictures of the church.[40]

The painting of the pulpit shows a sounding board designed to amplify the preacher's words. At the time the picture was painted the wall-paintings were still white-washed. It can be deduced that when the sounding board was erected, it was fixed to the wall but with no knowledge that the wall paintings existed: that accounts for the damage to the dragon's head.

*John Hassell's painting of the pulpit (copyright of Surrey History Centre)*

# CHARLWOOD CHURCH

*Charlwood church*    J Hassell

*Hassell's view of the church (above) and the font (below)*
*(copyright of Surrey History Centre)*

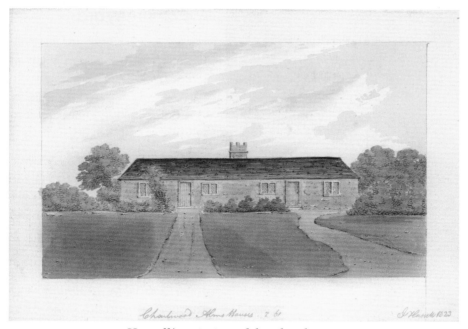

*Hassell's painting of the alms houses
(copyright of Surrey History Centre)*

Another painting by Hassell shows the view of the church from the north. The buttress on the north east corner is already there; so was the door into the chancel (now the vestry); and, of course, no Nicholas Room; otherwise it is little different to the view at present.

Baptismal fonts from Saxon to modern are almost always highly decorated: the font in Charlwood church is unusual in that it is plain stone, totally undecorated.[41]

At first sight one is perhaps inclined to dismiss the font as comparatively modern. The Hassell painting, however, shows it exactly as at present which proves that it was made before 1820: but when remains unknown.

Another Hassell painting shows alms houses in what is now part of the churchyard, near the Half Moon (with the church tower visible beyond). They were said to exist in 1786,[42] were shown on the 1842 Tithe Map, but removed at some time before the Ordnance Survey map of 1871.

*The yew tree, estimated to be over 1,000 years old*

## The Churchyard

The yew tree was dated in 1980 by a national tree expert as about a thousand years old. Sadly, in 2010, it was set alight, probably by youth smoking cigarettes. But half of it is still thriving.

The stone path is listed by Historic England in its own right as Grade II – as of historic interest. It is not known when it was laid down but the listing citation states:

*'Probably C17 or earlier. About 5 ft wide. Irregular slabs of Charlwood stone designed to protect churchgoers from mud. (cf. Parliamentary Survey of 1649-58 "the said pishe Church is situate from Horley 2 miles and from Leigh ffower miles or thereabouts and in the winter are very bad and dirty waives").*

Since the path is made of Charlwood stone it must have been laid at some time when the stone quarries were open, perhaps in the 1660s when the church tower was raised: the flag stones on the path being the bits of stone which were unsuitable for building.[43]

Lych gates were built at the entrance to a churchyard to provide a place for a coffin to wait out of the rain until a funeral service was about to begin. The Charlwood lych gate was built probably sometime in the 1700s.

It is sited in what appears to be a curious position,

*The lych gate*

not at the present entrance to the churchyard. That is because the original churchyard was only the part on the north of the path: the path was outside the churchyard.[44] In the 1920s the churchyard was extended, bringing in the area to the south of the path.

## The reordering

The Victorians had a great passion for rebuilding ancient churches. Nearby churches – Leigh, Betchworth, and St Bartholomew's at Horley – all suffered that fate. Charlwood is fortunate to have escaped.

With no great aristocratic families, we also escaped the church becoming dominated by carved stone memorials to long-forgotten patricians. We were also lucky that we escaped the tendency towards filling every window with stained-glass – over half our windows remain plain glass, letting in the sunshine and giving the whole church a light and spacious feel.[45]

Between 1860 and 1885, however, the complete internal layout of the church was changed.

- The altar was moved from the north aisle, where it had stood since c.1330, to the south aisle.
- The private pew belonging to the Saunders family was converted into choir stalls.
- New pews were installed throughout the church. In part of the south aisle the pews face each other across the aisle (as in a college chapel), this being the only configuration which prevents the congregation having their backs to the pulpit.[46]
- The chancel was converted into the vestry.
- The wall paintings were rediscovered – in 1858.
- Two musicians' galleries, one against the west wall (erected in 1716) and one against the north wall, were taken down.
- A new organ, made by the renowned George Holdich, was installed. It is still in good working order and is much commended by organ experts.

*William Burges*

These changes were made by Thomas Burningham, who was Rector from 1855 to 1884, advised by his friend, William Burges.

Burningham was keen on history, and was elected to the British Archaeology Council.

Burges was a well-known Victorian architect but somewhat eccentric. He was addicted to opium and enjoyed dressing in oriental costumes. He designed Cardiff Castle, Castell Coch and Cork Cathedral.

William Burges wrote up the discovery of the wall-paintings in an article in the *Archaeological Journal*. In it he described the paintings, indicated that some gave signs that they had been corrected by the artist, gave a sketch (with less detail than visible today), and observed that: '*it is true that they frequently err against anatomy and good drawing, yet, if we compare them with the subsequent productions of the fourteenth and fifteenth centuries, one cannot fail to be struck with a certain gracefulness and monumental severity displayed in the earlier works.*'

As a result of his friendship with Burningham, he also designed the church of St Michael and All Angels at Lowfield Heath in the parish of Charlwood. It was built in 1868 and remained a Chapel at Ease – served by the Charlwood rector or curate – until the 1970s when, following a change in local government boundaries, it was moved into the diocese of Chichester.

Burningham's wife, Mary Juliana, died in 1855, aged only 56, and he installed the stained-glass window above the altar in her memory.

Thomas Burningham suffered another sadness when his son, Edmund, died (in Winnipeg) aged 40. He is remembered in the small stained-glass window beside the main door. It contains an illustration of the martyrdom of St Edmund. Was it a coincidence that his son was christened Edmund, some twenty years before Thomas Burningham cleaned the whitewash off the wall-paintings, and revealed St Edmund – or at least the archer?

*The east window*

## Photography

By 1880 photography was just coming into use. George Wheatley, who lived at Charlwood House in the centre of the village, took over 100 photos of Charlwood houses and people. He is commemorated in the St George stained-glass window on the south wall which is described on page 47.

George Wheatley's photograph of Thomas Burningham with his son, Edmund, and daughter, Harriet, was taken in the early 1880s just before Edmund made his fateful trip to Winnipeg.

*Thomas Burningham with his son and daughter*

Wheatley's image, taken in the early 1880s, is the earliest known photograph of the interior of the church. Note the candles in the hanging pendant. Just visible are the stone tablets behind the altar containing the Creed, the Ten Commandments and the Lord's Prayer.

*The interior c.1880*

*The interior c.1910*

Above is another old photo, perhaps dating from around 1910. The candle pendant has been replaced by oil lights but candles remain on the pulpit and in the choir. The tablets appear to have gone. The photo below was taken in 1904. Note the chimney from the coal fire in the corner of the vestry (the fireplace is still there, behind a cupboard). Note also the old rectory. Otherwise there has been virtually no change in over 100 years.

*The exterior c.1904 showing the vestry chimney*

## The Rectory

A rectory has existed on the present site since the middle ages. Old maps show it as having a partial moat.[47]

A painting of the rectory was made by the then rector, William Ellis, in 1795. Soon after that, however, a new and larger rectory was built and was painted by Hassel in 1820. It is also pictured in the photo opposite taken by George Wheatley in the 1880s.

In those days rectors lived in style with a large contingent of servants, and stayed in office for a considerable number of years: Thomas Burningham was rector for 29 years; his successor, Edward Gibson, also for 29 years; and Grainger Thompson for 41 years. Gibson combined the job with being chairman of Reigate District Council for ten years. Grainger Thompson had lost an arm in the First World War, and alarmed the locals by driving erratically around the parish in an early Austin 7.

A full list of the rectors of St Nicholas' from 1242 onwards is given in *The Freemen of Charlwood.*[48]

*The rectory in 1795 (Ellis)*

*The rectory in 1820 (Hassell)*
*(copyright of Surrey History Centre)*

*The rectory in c.1880 (Wheatley)*

*The rectory fire, 1917*

The rectory was burnt down in 1917.[49] Many of the written records of church history were destroyed. The silver communion vessels melted but the silver was retrieved and recast to become the present chalice (cup) and patten (plate).

A new rectory was built in the 1920s. In 2015 the role of Rector was reduced to a part-time Priest-in-Charge, and in 2022 the Rectory was sold.

*The new rectory*

# The First World War, and since

The terrible impact of the First World War is recorded on the war memorial in the churchyard which contains the names of 52 men from Charlwood who died. Curiously it was during the war, in 1915, that the fine stained-glass window to the left of the pulpit was erected, in commemoration of George Wheatley and his wife, Mary. The choice of subjects reflects their Christian names: the left-hand panel shows St George slaying his dragon, and the centre panel depicts the Virgin Mary standing on a chess board – the analogy (from a 13th century tradition) being that, as the queen commanded the chess board so also Mary was Queen of Heaven.

The reredos behind the altar dates from 1935. The oak font cover, and the lectern, were presented in memory of Rector Grainger Thompson. The pews in the area under the tower were removed in around 1970.

In 1980 a Charlwood festival was held to mark the 900th anniversary of the church. Events included a jousting tournament and a visit by Princess Alexandra; also a week-long visit by some 40 American visitors from Texas who were invited to stay in some of Charlwood's medieval houses.[50] The funds raised were used to under-pin the south wall which was beginning to lean outwards.

*The reredos*

## Gatwick threats[51]

In 1952 the Government announced that Gatwick aerodrome would be expanded to two runways, with the northern runway, to be built first, pointing straight at Charlwood. That would have meant aircraft flying directly over the church, at a low height. However, after a vigorous protest campaign, the plans were amended so that the southern runway was built first, and angled away from Charlwood. The new runway was opened in 1956 and, having been extended, remains the main Gatwick runway. As air traffic increased, the noise became a problem in the church in the 1970s and 1980s, making it difficult to hear the sermon, but since then has diminished.

A more serious threat emerged in 1993 when the Government published diabolical plans for a second runway at Gatwick to the north of Charlwood which would have left the church sandwiched between the two runways. A massive campaign was organised which included a packed and televised protest meeting in the church, another church service at which a cabinet minister read the lesson, and, as an aid to press coverage, the restoration of the wall-paintings.

The result was to postpone a decision until 2003 when the plans were re-issued. Again Charlwood, and St Nicolas' church, would have been isolated between the runways. Another vigorous public campaign resulted in a government decision to rule Gatwick out.

In 2013, when the airport launched a new plan, backed-up with a colossal £40 million advertising and lobbying campaign, it was for a second runway to the south of the existing runway which would have had little direct impact on the church – except for proximity to a very large airport. It again was defeated. In 2019 Gatwick announced a plan to make full use of the already existing emergency runway.

The church was saved – at least until Gatwick decide to resuscitate their diabolical 1993 plan.

## The Nicholas Room

The need for a toilet had become urgent. With the advent of women clergy it was no longer possible to ask visiting priests to use the laurel bushes! And

*Cutting the first turf for the Nicholas Room, 2008,*
*showing where the boiler house has been demolished on the right.*

an increasing number of people who came by car to baptisms, weddings or funerals expected to find suitable facilities.

The church architect, Paul Sharrock, drew up sketch plans for ten different options, inside and outside the church. Those inside the church, which mainly involved putting an upper floor into the vestry or at the back of the church, all failed on the difficulty of sound-proofing the flush!

It was therefore decided to build onto the north wall of the church and, if a loo was to be provided, the plan might as well include a meeting room and a kitchen. It was realised that permission would never be granted if it was proposed to knock down part of an ancient wall: the door to the new extension had to be through the existing door from the vestry.

After intensive discussion by the church fabric committee and rejection of many different designs, a plan was produced in 2003 which met with general approval. But then the Government produced the plan for a potential runway at Gatwick, and it was realised that this would make it impossible to raise the necessary funds: it was a couple of years before progress could resume.

Building onto a Grade 1 listed building, of which the outside walls had not changed since 1480, involved extensive consultation. A faculty had to be obtained, an archaeological survey had to be undertaken, outline planning permission and, in due course, detailed planning permission, had to be obtained. All manner of conservation bodies had to be consulted.

Patrick Cox, the church treasurer, rightly insisted that the extension must be built in stone, and had the task of raising the necessary funds – over £400,000. The work was put out to tender and the contract was awarded to Riverside of Tonbridge. There is general agreement that they built both the walls, of Wealden sandstone from West Hoathly, and all the woodwork to a high quality.

Work started in summer 2008 and was completed in 2009. One box tomb, with an ornamental top-knot, was relocated. Under archaeological supervision, sixteen skeletons had to be removed from the site and later reburied. The new church room was 'christened' the Nicholas Room and has proved a valuable addition.

*The completed Nicholas Room*

## The church today

Just to bring the story up-to-date, in 2019 the church was rewired and new lights were installed at a cost of £130,000. It is good to record that the John Bristow and Thomas Mason Trust, that had grown out of the benevolence of the rector four hundred years ago, played a substantial part in financing both the Nicholas Room and the new lights.

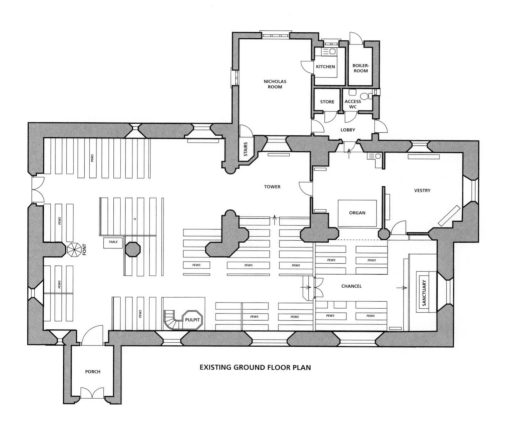

*A plan of the church in 2022*

# Appendix

## A speculative explanation of why Charlwood Church was built.

After the battle of Hastings in 1066 there was still a great deal of Saxon resistance. William marched first to Canterbury and then, his scouts reporting that the bridges over the Thames in London were stoutly defended, marched west along the North Downs to Winchester. From there he moved to Wallingford, and crossed the Thames in order to take London from the north – where he was crowned on Christmas Day 1066.

After Hastings the Saxons mounted a half-hearted rear-guard action, at a site not yet discovered by archaeologists, following which the remnants of Harold's army dispersed into the Weald. Williams of Poitiers, writing

in around 1070, describes how they fled from the battle '*some on horses they had seized, some on foot; some along roads, others through untrodden wastes.*'

Some may have slunk off home; others camped out in the woods. There they may have been joined by the stragglers from Harold's rapid march down from Yorkshire. Indeed it is recorded that at the battle of Hastings Harold had available only one third or one half of his intended force.

*The Battle of Hastings: scenes from the Bayeux tapestry*

The stragglers and survivors would have been horrified and enraged by the reports of the burning, looting, and rape carried out by the Normans. The Normans, according to one of the main historic sources, '*laid waste Sussex, Kent, Hampshire,*

52

APPENDIX

*Middlesex and Hertfordshire, and did not cease from burning townships and slaying men.*[52] The Domesday Book description, quoted on page 4, of how the cultivated land at Merstham was reduced to a quarter of its previous size fits that description.

Perhaps some remnants of the Saxon army eventually congregated in the woods and 'untrodden wastes' around Charlwood, and waged guerrilla war from there. Perhaps the name 'Ceorlwood' – the wood of men who owed allegiance to no lord – made it a natural place to rally, or perhaps the village acquired its name at that time.

In the five years after the Conquest, as is well documented, William had to undertake campaigns to subdue the Saxons in the West Country, in the north of England, in Herefordshire, and in Ely. The men of Kent *goaded by Norman oppression* plotted to seize Dover castle.[53]

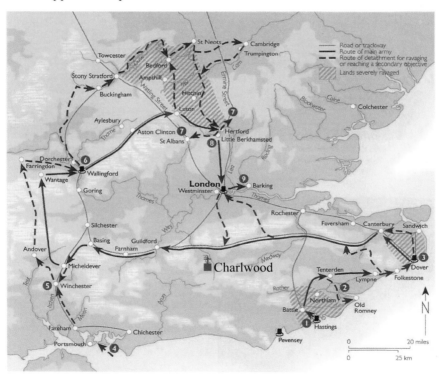

*William's route from Hastings to London.*
*The areas shaded red are those laid waste.*
*From* Campaigns of the Norman Conquest *(Matthew Bennett, 2001).*

There is no written evidence of a similar uprising in the Weald but it can be surmised that Charlwood became a centre for what would now be called 'insurgents', and that a contingent of Norman troops was sent down to round them up.

Afterwards, as happened elsewhere in England, the church would have been built by forced Saxon labour to impress and subdue the locals.

# Notes

1. The dendrodating system introduced in the 1990s. An early use of it was in Charlwood. Surrey Dendrochronology Project.https://dbrg.org.uk.
2. Hard limestone/sandstone, not the softer chalk of the North Downs. Reigate stone was also used in building the Tower of London in 1071
3. Malden HE (ed.) *Victoria County History: Surrey*. Volume 3, 1911. https://www.british-history.ac.uk/vch/surrey/vol3.
4. Bramber church was originally built as the chapel to the nearby castle. The tower was rebuilt in the 1700s.
5. The right to nominate the rector (the advowson), subject to the approval of the bishop, was held by various gentlemen from the 1500s to the 1900s. A full list is given in British History Online https://british-history.ac.uk.
6. *Domesday Book: Surrey*. 1975. Translation by John Morris. http://www.domesdaybook.co.uk/surrey.html.
7. Straker E. *Wealden Iron*. Bell & Sons, 1931.
8. Cleere H, Crossley D. *The Iron Industry of the Weald*. Leicester University Press, 1985.
9. Actually, if one draws careful lines on a map, they appear to lead to the wooden Saxon church (if my guess at its location is correct) or as some would say, straight to the Half Moon pub!
10. Gover JEB, Mawer A, Stenton FM. *The Place-Names of Surrey*. Cambridge University Press, 1934.
11. Barlow F. *Thomas Becket*. Weidenfeld and Nicolson, 1986.
12. The doors of rood screens therefore opened outwards: those of chantry chapels opened inwards.
13. Unfortunately his papers are at present not available.
14. Orderic Vitalis. *Historia Ecclesiastica*. All four volumes are available from various sources listed at https://catalog.hathitrust.org/Record/001407442
15. The older, original version of this story is about three students travelling away to school. They stopped in an inn and were drugged, robbed, and murdered. Over the years, especially in France and Western Europe, these grown male students came to be seen as little children. This is the most popular story in France, set to a well-known and beloved song. The image of Saint Nicholas with children in a tub at his feet is the most widespread image of the saint in Western Europe.

16. The feet of a second archer behind the main archer are just visible on the wall but he was not included in the Ann Worrall painting.
17. It has been speculated that perhaps only half of this painting had been finished when Richard Saunders died in 1480, and that work was halted when plans were drawn up for the extension of the south aisle.
18. Andre J Lewis FSA. *Surrey Archaeological Collections*, 1891.
19. Sewill R, Lane E. *The Freemen of Charlwood*. http://www. charlwoodsociety.co.uk/resources/The%20Free%20Men%20of%20 Charlwood.pdf pp 10-11.
20. The chancel is the area of a church in front of the altar, often with choir stalls.
21. Although the dendrodating system has established the exact dates of many Charlwood houses as between 1400 and 1600, it has failed – so far – to give a date for the various beams or rafters in the church.
22. Brayley E. *A Topographical History of Surrey*. Tilt & Bogue,1841.
23. Manning O, Bray W. *The History and Antiquities of the County of Surrey*. John White, 1814.
24. *The Freemen of Charlwood*. Ibid. p.48.
25. Burges (see page 40) thought that perhaps this wall also had wall-paintings on it.
26. *The Freemen of Charlwood* (ibid.) states (page 48) that these arches were restored in the bad architectural period of the 18th century.
27. John 15:1. 'I am the vine …'
28. *The Freemen of Charlwood*. Ibid. p.49
29. Edward Brayley writing in 1844 describes the Ten Commandments, the Lord's Prayer and the Creed as being placed over the screen, with the Royal Arms above. But I think this must have been an error – it would have been too top-heavy. A photograph in c.1885 shows them above the altar (page 52).
30. The post of King's Remembrancer still exists.
31. Henry VIII had wavered on churches having the Bible in English: sometimes against as allowing the common man to question the received wisdom; sometimes in favour in line with the new Protestant beliefs. In 1538 Thomas Cromwell ordered that an English Bible should be issued to every church but this order was partially rescinded in 1543. There is no record of when the Bible in English was first used in Charlwood.
32. *The Freemen of Charlwood*. Ibid. p.68.
33. Now stored in the Surrey Records Office in Woking.

34. When I gave my talks on church history in 2018-9, it was pleasing to have in the audience the Secretary of Earles Charity and four trustees of the John Bristow and Thomas Mason Trust.
35. John Walker *The suffering of the clergy*. 1714. Abridged version, Whittaker Rev R. *Wertheim*. Mackintosh and Hunt, London 1863. See also *The Freemen of Charlwood*. Ibid. p.113.
36. Aubrey J. *The Natural History and Antiquities of the County of Surrey*. E Curll, 1718.
37. Malden HE. *Victoria County History: Surrey*. Ibid.
38. *The Freemen of Charlwood*. Ibid. pp.114-115.
39. Edward Brayley in *A Topographical The History of Surrey* (ibid.), states that the sundial is inscribed '*Orate pro anima Thome Sander et Johanne uxoris ejus …*' But the *Victoria County History* (ibid.) says that this inscription was destroyed in the Civil War. It obviously refers to a memorial which existed before the sundial.
40. Now held at the Surrey History Centre.
41. Google has over 500 images of fonts: none of them are undecorated.
42. Malden HE. *Victoria County History*. Ibid.
43. There were also stone paths alongside many of the roads in Charlwood until the roads were widened in 1960 - 80. This might suggest a date in the 1850s, after the enclosure of the commons. *The Freemen of Charlwood*, however, states that the invoices found in the muniment chest included many for digging local stone to make 'Causeys' (causeways) dating from the late 1700s.
44. It belongs to the Surrey County Council and repairs are the responsibility of the Highways Department.
45. An example is St Nicholas, Bookham, the only other Grade 1 church in Mole Valley, which is dominated by Georgian memorials and rendered dark by an excess of stained glass.
46. E.W. Brayley, writing in 1841 (ibid.), had described the interior of the church as '*in a remarkably antiquated and rude style*' and the old pews as '*oak, very old and much shattered*'.
47. Shelley J. *History in Maps: Charlwood: A Parish on Weald Clay*. 2003. Maps of 1725, 1789 and 1840. Charlwood Society, 2003. (Out of print)
48. *The Freemen of Charlwood*. Ibid. p.179. Since Grainger Thompson retired in 1959, the Rectors have been Canon Alan Westrup to 1973, Canon David Clark to 1991, Bill Campen to 2015; and Priest-in-Charge Sue Weakley to 2021.

49. Photo from Shelley J. *Grandfather's Charlwood*. Charlwood Society, 1981. (Out of print)

50. An analysis showed what special attributes Charlwood had: Norman church, medieval houses and an airport. The airline British Caledonian put on a special flight from Houston and publicised the trip. As a result of the visit many long-lasting friendships were formed.

51. For a full description of Charlwood's battles against airport expansion, see Sewill B. *Tangled Wings*. 2nd edition 2020. https://www.aef.org.uk/uploads/2020/09/TANGLED-WINGS-2nd-edition-2020.pdf.

52. John of Worcester. *Chronicon ex Chronicus*. c.1100 - 30. Available at https://www.bsswebsite.me.uk/History/JohnofWorcester/Chronicle_John2.html.

53. Orderic Vitalis. *Historia Ecclesiastica*. Ibid.

# Index